the CRAZY world of MARRIAGE

Cartoons by
Bill Stott

EXLEY

Other books in the series:
The Crazy World of Birdwatching (Peter Rigby)
The Crazy World of Gardening (Bill Stott)
The Crazy World of Golf (Mike Scott)
The Crazy World of the Handyman (Roland Fiddy)
The Crazy World of Jogging (David Pye)
The Crazy World of Love (Roland Fiddy)
The Crazy World of Music (Bill Stott)
The Crazy World of Photography (Bill Stott)
The Crazy World of Rugby (Bill Stott)
The Crazy World of Sailing (Peter Rigby)
The Crazy World of Sex (David Pye)
The Crazy World of Skiing (Craig Peterson & Jerry Emerson)
The Crazy World of Tennis (Peter Rigby)

Published in Great Britain in 1987 by Exley Publications Ltd,
16 Chalk Hill, Watford, Herts WD1 4BN, United Kingdom.
Second printing March 1988
Third printing October 1988

ISBN 1-85015-077-X

Printed and bound in Hungary.

"It might make the world go round but it doesn't make it any tidier!"

"Your dancing hasn't changed since the first Beatles tour ..."

"Run away with my wife if you like, but if you value socks in pairs – forget it!"

"Say you love me."

"You love me."

"Well, if you haven't seen this show before, how come you rustle your paper in all the good bits?"

"You don't understand. I think Madonna's fantastic, ultimately sexy, amazing – a goddess – but I married you."

"Sorry about that, darling, I didn't want to miss the goal. You were saying something about having an affair ...?"

"When you said that your father was something in the city, I thought ..."

"Done? I haven't done *anything!"*

"We had this room on our first honeymoon ... Look, Paul, there's the very window-seat where you sang Will you love me tomorrow?"

"Why am I on the floor? Last night I tied the duvet to my big toe to stop you stealing it all. You're stronger than I thought."

"Well, there's nothing on TV and I feel like a good laugh. Why don't we get the wedding photos out?"

"I see he's got his Dad's hair ..."

"What do you mean if I was the only girl in the world?"

"I'd leave him if it weren't for the fact that he's the only one who can make the Christmas lights work."

"And when he does come to the supermarket, he's no help."

"Right, I've got my eyes closed. I just hope you haven't bought anything exotic this time – I can't abide your showy presents."

"Madam instructs me to say that if you don't want that chicken leg ..."

"You do as you're told, young man, or your mother and I will more than likely have an argument."

"Ease off, Dennis – these people are going to think we're not married."

"I'm just trying to imagine what you'll look like when you're 50, just in case I'm still married to you by then ..."

"The TV is broken. What is it to be – an argument or an early night?"

"I married him because I like the older man. Now he spends all his time trying to look younger ..."

*"Well, if you're as happy as your mother and I have been ...
Twenty-five years and never a cross word."*

WE DON'T TALK ANYMORE
GUESS WHO

"How come you can shave and wear a tie to go to that office you hate so much, but not when you spend the weekend with me?"

"George! Stop telling my joke."

"You really hate football, don't you?"

"I hate it when they take up a sport to be near you and turn out to be good at it."

"I don't love you after all. It turned out to be chronic indigestion .. "

"There must be some mistake. We're in credit!"

"At half the price, it would have looked fantastic."

"Okay, there's something wrong isn't there? I know the signs ..."

"You're not going to be masterful, are you? You always put your back out when you're masterful."

"I said 'Why don't you do something for me you haven't done in years?' He tried a headstand ..."

"... just cause or impediment why ..."

"Just because I can't remember what we were fighting about, doesn't mean I've forgiven you ..."

"Love is blind … drunk!"

"And the Lord have mercy on your soul. Ooops, turned over two pages there!"

"You want something to drive him mad? The effect or the bill?"

"Throw in another pig and I'll take her off your hands."

"You haven't a romantic bone in your body. Why can't you just ignore the greenfly?"

"Of course I'd really like to make it legal, but how do we know he's a real priest?"

"Furthermore I also promise to avoid such terms as 'the wife', 'her' or 'my better half'."

"You having another, Harry?"

"I see the Framlinghams had another fight."

"For heaven's sake, how many times have I told you about calling me at work?"

"I see the Framlinghams had another fight."

"For heaven's sake, how many times have I told you about calling me at work?"

"He thinks I love him for his come-to-bed eyes. Actually I'm crazy about the way he can't put shelves up."

"Sorry darling – you were saying something about how I don't notice you any more ...?"

"Don't tell me – you left early and gave the chauffeur the night off so that we could pull over and neck a little on the way back."

"Aah! A stiff breeze, a willing boat and the woman I love ...
Happy, darling?"

GONE TO
THERAPIST.
DINNER
NAILED
TO KITCHEN
CEILING

"My but you're magnificent when you're angry!"

"Casserole? Again?"

"Ha! Playing hard to get, eh?"

"The 'better' was okay while it lasted, but the 'worse' was really bad!"

"See his eyes flicker? You'd swear he understood every word I said!"

"The 'better' was okay while it lasted, but the 'worse' was really bad!"

"See his eyes flicker? You'd swear he understood every word I said!"

"Okay, a truck smashed into our bedroom. But admit it – just for a second you thought the earth moved!"

"What's a bigamist, Mother?"

"It's over then?"

"Hey Doreen – the guy on this TV counseling show just took a call from some woman who claims she hasn't had a meaningful conversation with her husband in 16 years ... Doreen?"

"I know I said it
with music in Majorca;
but this is not Majorca,
I'm freezing and there's
a policeman coming."

"You may be a mediocre lover, but nobody scratches a back like you do!"

"You might think it's full of olde worlde charm, but I'll tell you – after an hour every night for the last 23 years, maybe you'd find it a little tedious."

"I wish my folks were like yours and hated pop music ..."

"Flirting? Who was flirting? I was trying to start an affair!"

"Ok, ok, you win. Your paper-hanging is better than mine."

"Get back on your pedestal instantly, woman."

"It's my turn to have the headache."

"The old fool insisted on an anniversary waltz – and locked solid!"

"Of course the life insurance is paid up … why?"

"You romantic old thing, you!"

"That ideal man you sorted out for me? It's worn out. Got any more?"

"Her hand in marriage? Sure! You wouldn't consider taking the rest of her, would you?"

"And Stephen's heavily into conservation and anti-blood sports, aren't you darling?"

"Yes, I've come back – but only because Hugo can't settle at my mother's."

"So this big mean-looking kid walks up and says 'Gimme the bag'. And Gerry says 'Okay punk, beat it', didn't you Gerry?"

"Does the best man have the safety pin?"

"No problem, officer – it's just foreplay!"

"Sorry officer, but this was where it all started. The first time this was a cornfield."

"And that's the Hopkinsons – they have some really good fights."

"No dear ... Yes dear ... Pick your mother up? Yes dear ...
Mow the lawn? Yes dear ... No dear ..."

"Last week they promised to pay me a fine each time they forgot to put something away. By now, I could afford a new video!"

"... a big woman, around 230 pounds, loud voice, badly fitting dentures and a slight moustache. And do me a good turn, son – don't try too hard ..."

"Well I'm glad it's not <u>my</u> husband making a fool of himself!"

"But I do still love you. It's just your clothes, politics, conversation and habits I want you to change."

"Wait a minute – we agreed. Tuesday is my day to moan about the office!"

"He gave me the best years of his life. As it happened they weren't fantastic, just the best he could do."

Other books in the series:

The Crazy World of Birdwatching. £3.99. By Peter Rigby. Over eighty cartoons on the strange antics of the twitcher brigade. One of our most popular pastimes, this will be a natural gift for any birdwatcher.

The Crazy World of Gardening. £3.99. By Bill Stott. The perfect present for anyone who has ever wrestled with a lawnmower that won't start, over-watered a pot plant or been assaulted by a rose bush from behind.

The Crazy World of Golf. £3.99. By Mike Scott. Over eighty hilarious cartoons show the fanatic golfer in his (or her) every absurdity. What really goes on out on the course, and the golfer's life when not playing are chronicled in loving detail.

The Crazy World of The Handyman. £3.99. By Roland Fiddy. This book is a must for anyone who has ever hung *one* length of wallpaper upside down or drilled through an electric cable. A gift for anyone who has ever tried to "do it yourself" and failed!

The Crazy World of Jogging. £3.99. By David Pye. An ideal present for all those who find themselves running early in the morning in the rain and wondering why they're there. They will find their reasons, their foibles and a lot of laughs in this collection.

The Crazy World of Love. £3.99. By Roland Fiddy. This funny yet tender collection covers every aspect of love from its first joys to its dying embers. An ideal gift for lovers of all ages to share with each other.

The Crazy World of Music. £3.99. By Bill Stott. This upbeat collection will delight music-lovers of all ages. From Beethoven to Wagner and from star conductor to the humblest orchestra member, no-one escapes Bill Stott's penetrating pen.

The Crazy World of Photography. £3.99. By Bill Stott. Everyone who owns a camera, be it a Box Brownie or the latest Pentax, will find something to laugh at in this superb collection. The absurdities of the camera freak will delight your whole family.

The Crazy World of Rugby. £3.99. By Bill Stott. From schoolboy to top international player, no-one who plays or watches rugby will escape Bill Stott's merciless exposé of their habits and absurdities. Over 80 hilarious cartoons – a must for all addicts.

The Crazy World of Sailing. £3.99. By Peter Rigby. The perfect present for anyone who has ever messed about in boats, gone pea-green in a storm or been stuck in the doldrums.

The Crazy World of Sex. £3.99. By David Pye. A light-hearted look at the absurdities and weaker moments of human passion – the turn-ons and the turn-offs. Very funny and in (reasonably) good taste.

The Crazy World of Skiing. £3.99. By Craig Peterson and Jerry Emerson. Covering almost every possible (and impossible) experience on the slopes, this is an ideal present for anyone who has ever strapped on skis – and instantly fallen over. "A riotous suggestion ... very funny and very original." (The Good Book Guide)

The Crazy World of Tennis. £3.99. By Peter Rigby. Would-be Pat Cashes and Chris Everts watch out.... This brilliant collection will pin-point their pretensions and poses. Whether you play yourself or only watch on TV, this will amuse and entertain you!

United Kingdom
These books make super presents. Order them from your local bookseller or from Exley Publications Ltd, Dept BP, 16 Chalk Hill, Watford, Herts WD1 4BN. (Please send £1.00 to cover post and packing.)

United States
All these titles are distributed in the United States by Slawson Communications Inc., 165 Vallecitos de Oro, San Marcos, CA92069 and are priced at $8.95 each.